The Watcher

The Watcher

Poems

Agnes Eva Savich

Cedar Leaf Press
San Antonio, Texas

Cedar Leaf Press
17503 La Cantera Parkway, Suite 104-240
San Antonio, TX 78257

First edition

Library of Congress Cataloging-in-Publication Data

Savich, Agnes Eva [1976]

The Watcher: Poems
p.   cm.

ISBN   978-0-9820413-4-5 (paper)

Library of Congress Control Number: 2009940815

1. Savich, Agnes Eva [1976]. 2. Poetry—Free verse.
3. Poetry—Contemporary. 4. Poetry—Love.
5. Generation X

This book was printed on acid-free paper in the United States of America.

For S.S., M.S., and R.S.

The Watcher

Contents

Section Five: Roots

Section One

Fruit

The Watcher

Miles Davis "In a Silent Way"

Molasses dawn: the spread of thick Van Gogh light
A lone reflective swan glides slowly to and fro
Softly drawling trails over honey waters in its wake
Against the backdrop of fat castle towers

A trumpet
(Lips and golden mouthpiece, illuminated warm and
blurred)
Expels its viscous honey through the land
While through triangular windows strange roads twist away
The world a listening still life at the wrought iron gates

Old lady pushes her saucy grey cart down the road
She's got *her* groceries
Piled high as the grey bun atop her crocheted form
A pigeon careens drunkenly above
The rhombuses of housetops in cubistic layers

Distant villages teem with pointillist life
The studded particles of each carefully placed note
Merging seamlessly into their inhabitants
A shimmering dance of daytime hues

Until the canvas yields to afternoon sounds
Their rain falls gently from the towers
Into the viscid purples down below
Concentric orbs quivering from each slow-motion droplet

Fluid clocks chime their fluctuating non-hours
The gentle lullaby descends
And with the last light's blessing through the droplets

The Watcher

A rainbow arches sweetly over all
The castle fades to ebony and silence
An island in an ink-black pool
The window panes reflecting
Calmly as they always have.

Drunkenness

Infernal sound of rushing pixels
through which bulbous faces push
like fat blood cells
in collateral transit
waxing, looming up, then waning

Conversation is a vain correspondence
Speaking is a fast blurred tunnel
with flapping lips on either end
Phrases squirm out
from the black depths
and flap out singularly.

Gradually the sound pixels take over
The vein no longer connects
Suddenly only the inner darkness
As apprehension collects
This alienation, this Big Brain
with pixels for friends:
a ghost tuned inward.

Creating Eden

in the garden
our walls melt

we dig deep
in each other's soil

you root in me
i bloom

we are spiraling
humid winds

i breathe you in
you exhale me

our touch defines
the soft faces of petals

my curve of waist lands
your smooth shoulder

we are the sun
always beyond the storm

the fire that welds
by God's hand

two souls together
into paradise

Cycles

boredom born of mindless procrastination
listening listlessly to washing machine churn
with only thoughts of wet towels
extinguishing the spark of better projects

limpness of limbs unmoved by lovemaking
for weeks now, months
a patient silent stained glass mosaic
where my heart is supposed to be

the fibers of forgotten lust
secretly dry-cleaning somewhere
to arrive someday like a comet
entangling me on the floor or the bed or...

i can imagine the warmth
i can taste the fragrance
my body remembers somewhere the feeling
now ignored upon a shelf in coiled folds

even the washing machine
knows how to throb wetly when turned on
its steady rhythm mocks me with the old lie:
that a young pretty girl can get it when she wants.

Hum

Hum
along, coworker
to the music on my pc
Off-key
your mindless drone
a fly
buzzing in my ear
but just discretely
barely above
the volume
whether it
be high or low
as if
i wouldn't know
it's you

i have tried
adjusting
yet your little moans
rise and fall
with it
your voice box
i fear
has a mind
of its own

and i try
to pretend
hushlittlebaby
ancientwoman
grandmothercroon

The Watcher

but
no, the drone
distinguishes not
from classical
to heavy metal
or techno

i'm too nice
to let you know
there's an army
at my ear
fighting off
each
MmmmHhhh
and
HhhhMmmm

Concrete Jungle

Ensconced in a corner branch
fluorescent vines creep overhead
the filtered air is filled with the cacophony
of chitter-chattering mouths
sporadic bursts of clicking sounds
and the shrill shrieks of telephones

Outside, in the concrete jungle paths
squares of light flash from glass leaves
in calculated photosynthesis of business.
Below, the yellow beasts roam,
stop to swallow their prey,
then charge away with the herd.

With animal spirits our bodies perch, rigid,
free to roam only at the morning's rush
and back again with the evening's silvery stream
caged by choice of necessity
yet yearning for unfettered air

Beneath an endless canopy of ceilings
each worker-bee drones insulated from the sun:
A shadow among shadows.

The Watcher

Grandmother!

that we should come to this
bodies dependent
on machines designed by calculating minds

heart beating to electronic stimuli
mapped by four different graphs
for noise, strength, beat, frequency

lungs pumped by air tubes
taped into mouth and nose
hurtling down the throat

she gave birth to my mother
who gave birth to me
who watched her frail body last night

hearing "stable condition", i kissed her forehead
and hummed her favorite Christmas tune ten times
to the rhythm of the monitors: her heart

but in my mind of mortal fears
i forever see her numbly twitching
morphine-encumbered

i see her hand rising to her sealed mouth
then falling back again
the tear wetting her closed upturned eye

my own heart pounding in my chest
i see the tube-pierced carotid pulsing
the iodine and blood rivulets drying

The Watcher

the length of her pale legs
and where they cut the veins:
four pieces for her heart: four arteries out.

i see her waking sometime in the night
fists feebly beating against the walls of pain
consciousness a lonely muffled roar

that we should come to this
the survival of the beloved body: mechanized
in the hands of clipboard-checking strangers.

Numb Monday

Blank, as the edges of this page
A poet muses, melancholy
Over another Monday's wasted hours
Working for the bare necessities
Of clothing, food, electric power

Lacking courage to un-tether
From the green teat of Full Time Stability,
The mouse finds its cheese again and again
In that boundless virtual maze
Gazing off, dazed, every now and then

Doodling self-employment pipe dreams
While completing tasks by rote
The poet's weariness a heavy something
Numbs the whole being into blankness
All is filtered through this noise of nothing.

The Watcher

And It Is Already the Middle of Another April

Time relentless time
What mystery drives
Its accelerating pantomime?

Crawling on all fours,
It was concerned with creation
Gesturing expansive, slow
Its face as brilliant
As the sun

Each year as biped,
It quickens
Rendering yesterdays more distant
Its countenance mocking
As we reel

As three-legged creature
It will blaze
With speed of plunging meteor
Until it takes
A final bow

Fatigue Is

the seductive song of sleep
waxing over consciousness

fighting the dead weight of eyelids
no Ulyssean toothpicks can uphold

the softness of limbs
against unrelenting angles

time tapped out by ever growing fingernails
on surfaces too hard to be pillows

the gnawing bite of late nights
on tomorrow's shoulder blades

a spine finding solace in fetal position
wilting again and again and again

dreams deferred to the shriveling light of day
a heavy jam crusting upon skin

slack-jawed with a mouthful of worries
the tongue, like Sisyphus, tired of rolling out words

Wisdom Tooth

Jutting iceberg tip
stubbornly refusing
to fall in line behind the others
jostling molars for dominance
no matter how many
times the tongue
flaps back to break up the fight
Stupid tooth
chiseling in from gummy depths
useless, yet
tenaciously heralding
irrevocable older age

Housewife's Lament

hello silence
i want to kick up my heels
in the empty room of you
its mirrored walls
echoing nothing
and nothing back again

each fuzzy-slippered footfall
will not make an impression
in the black soundlessness
when i fall on my knees
or arch back on my elbows
the fleece robe will muffle

smothered from head to foot am i
my dance will not break
the silence pressing on my ears
pressing in my mind
releasing only baby-babble
for so many months i've forgotten—

how to speak

The Sandman's Mistake

Five hours is not enough sleep
I feel disjointed—heavy lids

if they could cry
it would be globules of honey

droop, my heavy head
loll over like a buttercup
too full of morning dew

Mr. Sandman, why have you left
behind these bags?

now somebody across the world
will have insomnia

while I must carry
this excess of slumber
throughout the day.

Carpe Diem

concentrate on the convulsive skiphop of the record
there, mallets fall dominoeing into slots
now the crackling sound of time cooking
the universe is skillet shaped, take that, physicists!
bodily rolling calm with all the nerves waving as a tattered
banner
each stream manifested on a different frequency of sound
time pulses as the universe's heartbeat
gently rolling over all space; calm; ever unfolding
catalyzing mad shimmering tremors of which
sound and gravity are but two of the wonders it bestows

rhythm knocks into the real room on wooden horse legs
intruder! companion! slithering glider! stamper!
oh to fly with fingers over letters as over notes:
this stream is composed of a long chain of singular icons
string of consciousness—I weave letter beads in a line
a steady arrow weaving, spearing through the fundamental
blocks
yet this H this Y are somehow related to my thoughts
they are the first visible signs outside the black tunnel
the light coming in immediately recognizable pinpoints

always the music of silence

AND NOW THE THUMP OF MODERNITY ENTERS THE ROOM
metropolis thrusts up one erection after another
electric lights beam in grid formation and pattern the air
steel, glass: they wrap in angled whip cracks around each
rising form
sheathing the solidity and electricity within

The Watcher

thump in underground caves of bodies pulsing
finding the cosmic pulse
but does it have a soul? a dinosaur one, perhaps
crude and large and loud yet basic and
ab ovo. here I sit sprung up from a molecule
now with my own ears I breathe the earth of my
forefathers
with my own eyes I feel the trees they planted
with my own touch I can hear the wind they heard

now castle-dark in deep mahogany corridors and flashing
wisps
this is a strange union: man and instrument
one plays the other; a truly reciprocal duo
in the end, the two merge into one concept; neither man
nor horn
but as sound creating itself in a great vacuum
woven succession of singularities
yet this B-flat this D are somehow related to my thoughts
they are the soft pillars of the tunnel

it is a painting unlike any other

Ashtray

Graveyard
home to so many
extinguished thoughts

Crystal coffin
of slender nothings

Once such heroes
released ethereal wisps...

Late night liquor seekers'
salvation.

Bad Trip (The Spirit Warrior)

There are Good forces
and there are Evil forces

Begin with breathless wonder:
Something goes to sleep and something wakes

Enormous yawns unlock the ears, the chest
slowly shadows come to life
wide, flat surfaces breathe
straight lines show their true nature as sine waves
and the ground click-clacks in interlocking pieces

Cyclical as breath,
pathways narrow and widen
birdglints of butterlight shimmerglide
breath halls susurrate throat-warmly

blink,
time code shows through the cracks of space
ping,
another tiny blue portal fades away
points of light attach to retina,
swinging to and fro
the wave of arm
        (arm)
                (arm)
                        (arm)
ten
one hundred
snakefingers
paint the canvas of the airspace

The Watcher

Shaman-woman, sit and breathe the earth of forefathers
grass a childlike joy upon the palm
bound by gravity upon one speck in a vast universe
contained in this body
        This body
        This Body

This Body
it breathes
it pounds
it thinks

It sweats
it swallows
it pees
it sees

does it breathe?
yes it breathes
docs it pound?
yes it pounds
yes it pounds
yes it pounds

feel it red,
feel the muscle
as an organ,
as it gallops
in its cage

black blood

black blood weakens the body:
a sudden wrench in the works

The Watcher

thoughts loop loop thoughts
the relentless sequencing
(does it pound? yes it pounds.
does it breathe? yes it breathes)

But the brittle sound of red-lipped, chomping jaws fills the
room
a swarm of them flies overhead,
sounding their dry laughter

Everything invades everything else,
out of control
ceiling tiles
drip down,
please,
no,
enough!

turn OFF
this x-ray which bares
the roiling, blood-swollen, amorphous mass within
sweep OUT
the haunted hall
where the skeletal hag slowly creaks, spider-webbed inside
unTANGLE
the cassette tape of time
being eaten by Radio Irrational

hah, glass of juice? it is worse:
grandfather clock in a vacuum;
brain a lugubrious pendulum
that just
might stop

The Watcher

Forever.

NO! Enough!

cast OUT:
>the writhing worms
>the churning bile
>the blackened stumps
>the gaping mouths

slow DOWN:
>the hands of time
>the chains of thought
>the speed of heart
>the fears of death

And it breathes in and out
doesn't fade, doesn't die

A single object
(twig...
glass of water...
cup of tea...)
becomes the ferryman's bribe
to turn back from the underworld

The hellish tunnels of fractals gone mad
gradually become
a gentler rain of pixels;
a geometric language quietly decoding behind closed lids

An exhausted softness blankets the Spirit Warrior
Every limb and thought falls back in line
to its rightful place

The Watcher

And purpose

Something wakes and something goes to sleep
End with breathless wonder

Once again, Good has triumphed over Evil
Good will always triumph over Evil.

Section Two

Leaves

In Lust I Trust

you created me as a lover
under your wildness
I learned the holy pleasures
of losing control

in that first year
our daily lovemaking
became
my daily bread

you created me as a lover
gave me my first
transubstantiation
from mere human to vibrating angel

we prayed deeply
in each other
offering and receiving
wet libations

you created me as a lover
like furtive animals
tumbling off the bed
never satiated

our altar floated
from bath to futon
to bed where we
worshipped each other

you created me as a lover

The Watcher

in white noise ecstasy
murmured from my lips:
God's name softly.

The Way Our Bodies Fit Together

the way bread slices cling to make the loaf
how a scoop of ice cream fills a bowl
and an orange rind clings to the fruit

the way incense smoke canopies a room
how clean soap lingers on the skin
and perfume wraps the mind in a cloud

the way a painting dances while still
how a kaleidoscope aligns again
and the ivory calla lily curves softly

the way a chord layers together perfect notes
how silence gives meaning to music
and favorite songs can make you feel

how fluently two hands always lock
and lips seal from every angle:

the way our bodies fit together

Gray Sky

The light forgot to fade last night,
attests this morning's dimness
Pale gray-blue backdrop to dirty rain
clouds thick as cigarette smoke
smother each building from view

Unfocused I gaze through office windows
No golden ray dares pierce
the day's stormy shroud
Sleep creeps into my mind
as grayness sweeps the outside.

I'd rather run to the hills
hand in hand with you, hair streaming
shedding sleep, stupor, and monotony—
faces stung by wet flecks
we, the sunshine of the storm.

The light, unchanging, meets its twin—
upon twilight's doorstep they merge
this gray day becomes evening again
and I will slink through streets
towards that warm glow of home

Solder

your sensual force
is a chemical I choose to ingest
you unveil your masterpiece
in heavy ambush
to electrically baptize me

come down unto me
rise up and make my hair fly
I lay awake and silent
dying for you
besiege me not once but fifty times

breathe me in
ignite my core
sublimate me
I'll evaporate into kinetic sound
let my hair fly like a melody

into the miracle of the moment
quivering we'll sail
become tempestuous
heard by the sun
reminding her to open toward Earth

and when I am enflamed
into a golden web
my bones trembling like crystal
my need will be victorious:
for you to solder into my veins

Places

Climb up a narrow ladder
to the barn
when everyone's asleep
animals rustling somewhere below
a thick blanket
spread upon the straw
the smell of it everywhere
like clover and spring fields
the hay dust would rise
in the moon light
as you opened me
and drove me
into the soft hard bales

Pull over on a long highway
road trip out west
with miles before and after us
sticking to the backseat
where we might even sleep
feet against windows
in the cup holder
while we gave the car
a story inside
worthy of the drive
for private memories
of our crazy young years

Lay on a deserted beach
right in the spot
where the breaking waves
would lap our hips

The Watcher

locked together
surging forward
the ocean making love to ours
or bobbing in the shallows
shooting up to the stars
through me
making earthquakes
down over you

Coyly stretch in bed
with black satin sheets
and candles blazing all around
slow pulsating
red lights on the ceiling
the center of the vortex
of the universe's chaos
focused into
the deepest joining point
of our souls and bodies
fulfilling the middle pillar
of life's trilogy:
birth, orgasm, and death
alone together
forever in the moment
that fifth dimension:
lust in the depth of time
simply lover and lover.

The Watcher

Oh to paint my lover's laughter

Oh to paint my lover's laughter upon canvas
I'd blend plump tumbling red berries
with *altocumulus undulatus* in the sky

Or to capture by infrared impression
the sculpted curves of our embrace
the soft lush blurs of negative space
between two perfectly melded forms

Oh to compose a symphony of his touch
Tumultuous string adagio, a violoncello solos
Over the resonant tympani of my heart

Or one lone oboe traces a note
seductively upon airspace, time, my arm
trailed by the warm breath of clarinets
and tender intertwining of flutes.

The Nap

your face
turning up from sleep
nestled in my arm
i struggle with the other
for my camera
to save its sweetness
kissable dewdrop
captured in a ray of sun
and shutter's snap

One of Those Poems

I see the moon rise in your eyes
Cool sheath of light
Guiding my way
I see the sun set in your palm
Putting the day
in your back pocket
Your heart holds the earth
precious, close,
yours to take.
Give me your vision, your hands, your heart
So that I may
have the world, too.

Love for Breakfast

I love unwrapping you
like a cinnamon bun
in the morning
warm, toasty, and coiled

special softness
sweet innocence
reserved for my senses
to discover each day

I peel back the covers
your sleepy limbs
heavy with sleep
pull me to you

where I stick
nuzzling in the warmth
tasting love
in morning light

The Watcher

capturing your essence

you are the smooth underbelly
of a water drop—
shiny and cute,
the perfect morning bath for a wood nymph
(such as I)

you are the cat's paw, de-clawed
still and perfect,
gentle and neat
curled up just so
that when I look at you
you make my soul feel the same

you're a winding river
bordered by gnarly trees
with all the shades of green
upon which, on a perfect day,
the sun dappling through the canopy,

I float peacefully
in a canoe
wearing a white dress
with a pretty umbrella

you are the kitten's purr
warm and faithful
snuggly-soft
hugging my senses
in unwavering whirrs of love

you are the bright face of a daffodil

The Watcher

drawing my face near
irresistibly
for a petal smooth kiss
your face beaming sunshine

you are the melt of chocolate in the mouth
overwhelmingly sweet
slowing time
to deliciousness
savoring the eternity of the moment
with a happy tongue

you are the cool mountain stream
and the mountain
and the sun shining down on them
on one of those fresh days
where all the joy of life
is renewed

you are the last echo of a chord
just sung by a choir
in a cathedral
with the most beautiful
arched ceilings and stained glass
you're that soft sound
that fills my cells
in the spaces between nuclei
before anyone claps or speaks,
when all is air and echo,
all is wonder and emotional peak.

The Watcher

Drifting and luscious

Drifting and luscious
She suddenly found
the room confining
as she realized herself.
This self awareness
was almost too much—
the sheer desire to be,
well, consumed
made her weak
Spinning, and oh how
her mind drifted
A need to gorge herself
but food (though
certainly available)
was not the answer.

The Weeping Willow's Desire

The willow at the lake's edge
seduces him with long flowing strokes
come into my roots
she pleads
caressing his surface with her tiny leaves
the wind gives me thirst
for it makes me dance
an eternal primal sway
awakening the root of me

The willow at the lake's edge
tries with all her limbs
seep into my core
she beseeches
you are swollen from the rains
don't you need to touch the shore?
there to enter by the grasses
and saturate my innermost nexus
with your excess

The lake beside the willow
laps the crevices between her surface roots
the gods wept at your beauty
he explains
to create me here beside you
for each of your rings
I will grow bigger
sinking deeper towards your center
in eternal symbiosis

The willow at the lake's edge

The Watcher

feels these whispers at her base
grow timeless with me then
she nods
and so by grass, into moist earth
down to her taproot, up her trunk
she shimmers as his lapping words
spread through her synaptic branches
until she undulates for evermore.

Triptych for a Bride

Intoxication
As though the salty sea air
Permeates your mind

—

Coy, uplifting smiles
Blushing, trap the breath midway
In expectation

—

Having found the one
Whose arms forever hold you
In a warm cocoon

Longing

I listen to music
to fill the space of your absence
every note plucks the strings of my emotions
each change of chord
another deeper level of missing

melodic sadness
the distance from my touch to your body
were it to travel at the speed of sound waves
I could caress you now
as the sound pours through me

each instrument
becomes a different part of you
vocals kiss my face
guitars encircle me in their embrace
the bass enters me steadily

come back
across the country with your love
play upon my skin
not phantom chords
but the duet of our reunion.

Harem

Where spirits lay in smoke-filled chambers
Languidly awaiting the entrance of pleasure
Sighing, pushing locks of hair tenderly from brows
Glistening lightly with small beads of sweat
Palm fronds rest immobile in their ornate pottery

Chiffon curtains billow, rippling in the candlelight
Each flame cupped in demi-spheres of glass
Sending shadows dancing seductively upon walls
Hips swaying convulsively, repetitively on wicks
While small plumes rise in lines converging on ceiling tiles

Lips part, and hands slide down smooth bodies
Not allowed to touch each other until the master comes—
Sheathed in white and leather, full of urge
To spear the soft depths of many bodies, waiting
Waiting for the parting and the entrance in the night

Coy looks exchange across the flagstone floors
Each four-cornered station softer than the next
Breasts shift beneath their wrapped silk veils
As thighs haul over thighs in restless lounging
Feet bejeweled in hammered gold and gems

Musky odors permeate the air in sweet seductive wafts
A nipple grazed absentmindedly by braid's tip
Blushes and hardens momentarily in annoyance
Yet still the master does not come;
He sups in merriment with his finest men

A yawn, and the youngest of them falls to sleep

The Watcher

The rest in stages daydream themselves into a trance
So concentrated that the master's entrance
Does not cause a ripple or a sigh or a glance
His eyes fall upon the newest and the youngest in her
sleep

With smoldering eyes he stealthily glides into her bed
One gentle hand in silence peels the silk away
And grazes on the very ends of peachy down along her
form
In dream, her turning face reveals the smoothest curve of
jaw
Aroused, the master plunges a fingertip into her softest
place

A moan, the young one wakes into her nakedness
The rush of manly presence dials her senses high
Before she blinks he enters her with stunning force
Then slows to let her powers expand and flow
Her role she slips into with grace and measured sensuality

Each thrust and she is coiled perfection
The human half of his projected desire
Their bodies connect as the electricity and the plug
Through an interface; the center sphere into which they
converge
A ring of fire – a ring of light – a ring of glistening gold

Their hot cocoon of breath a bellows in the room
Pulsing wicks and sending currents of air across the others
Brows spring awake and slowly crawl in unison across the
floor
And hands entwine into the two, becoming four and six
His white robes are slowly lifted then wildly flung away

The Watcher

The velvet sheets crease, rippling ridges fall and rise
The pleasure of a single multi-limbed organism in heat
Gathers momentum as it writhes in kaleidoscopic motion
Arms graze curves graze knees graze napes graze hair
Crescendoing into a chorus of symbiotic sighs

Then stillness and the giant butterfly's wings unfold
Each body a stripe of color in the exhausted pattern
The candle wicks extinguish in hot melted pools
Night breezes carry away the lingering scents of incense
The sated master slips away, five bodies still entwined.

Section Three

Branches

Metaphors for Growing a New Human Being

Two parallel timelines
one jump-started by a spark
the other continuing from the depth of a past
that existed before the new one

A quantum leap
into existence
from two previously unrelated elements
the Big Bang of new life

A twinkling universe
of neurons, cells, thoughts
encased in a soft sphere
inside another universe

An unheard cry
building momentum
while the established pattern of chatter
continues its patter

Tabula Rasa
all the wonder of discovery
that the nurturer cannot but relive
in painting it

Two foremost links
of a winning chain of evolution
only to be added onto
as long as time is

Supernova in the Dark

seed of wisdom,
kernel of light
supernova in the dark

first traveling
from far apart
through thin filaments
to make the jump
and lie in wait

seed of wisdom,
kernel of light
supernova in the dark

waiting
squirming
piercing
maybe confirming
in the morning

seed of wisdom,
kernel of light
supernova in the dark?

will know if true
if there's a pink line
in window #2

Cravings: A Poem Pregnant with Humor

Oh sauerkraut, oh sauerkraut
how tasty are your juices
a forkful here, a forkful there
devoured by the bowlful

and in the next moment
an orange catches my eye
no, maybe two
peeled slowly & savored

the hours pass
the fridge-wonderland beckons
kraut—I must hide it from
that top front shelf

I reach beyond
for creamy cottage cheese
plain, the little curds
playing on my tongue

the yearning
for acidity returns
a pineapple chunks snack cup
does the trick

the days pass
my husband complains
of prison-food dinners:
beans & rice, cheese & broccoli

I retaliate
with red borscht soup

and mushroom dumplings
with sauerkraut on the side

68

Urban Love Reality

Overcast afternoon
my husband & I
both jobless
and with colds
sit together
in different rooms:
his electric guitar
sends out tendrils
my poetry
tries to capture the moment

this was my college love-seeking fantasy
true love as I dreamed it to be
the way it was meant for me

Starving artists
with a baby on the way
a house waiting in Texas
with real trees
moving far
from this concrete jungle
sirens blare by
while we create
above the same hardwood floor
an urban love reality

this was my
college love-seeking fantasy
true love as I dreamed it to be
the way it was meant for me

ninth month haiku trio

ninth month
the sun bursts through
storm clouds

so swollen she sweeps little leaves into piles

ninth month
the sun's face looms
on the horizon

Birthing Moon

rain-heavy sky
I feel another contraction
coming on

moonlight
through the blinds
she crowns

fireplace blazing
another Scorpio
is born

lunar eclipse
soft cooing
from our newborn

turning the clock back—
her tiny fingers
tiny toes

full moon
the absence of
my big round belly

starry night
I realize a mother
was born too

mother-daughter moments

72

ma-ma
as she touches my face
first narcissus

mother and daughter
each in her own thoughts
fireflies

night nursing—
how small the earth
in the universe

The Watcher

in this slice of life

in this slice of life
there are perfect sunny spring days
pink blossoms on black branches
stand out against bright blue
baby hair rises softly in the breeze
as mommy rocks the green hammock

there is morning light
through pink corduroy curtains
and busy coos from the crib
soon cold little hands and feet
will snuggle up to a breast
and warm up as the milk flows

every day there is music
tiny hands explore the keyboard
connected to daddy's computer
laying down multiple tracks—
the five-month-old's masterpiece!
an ambient odyssey

daddy plays guitar, they're both
singing "I'm a poopy little baby,
I'm a poopy little girl, I'm a poopy little baby,
poopin all over the world"
this original composition
silliness for baby's delight

Gymboree, mommy-baby yoga,
playgroup with the north mamas
playgroup with the south mamas
an explosion of activity

The Watcher

where babies smile at each other
and mamas try to connect

cloth diaper changes—
soft fleece and rows of plastic snaps
pink or black or violet or green froggies
vocalizing, funny faces to the lights
writhing little naked baby
pressing her toes into her mouth

all day long that sweet face
turns to her mother for nourishment
how the little ankles cross
and how deeply she moans and sighs
when she sucks the milk out
in her nook across mommy's lap

in this slice of life
bedtime is a sea of milk
enough to last til morning
pink lamplight recreates the womb
Mediterranean lullabies keep time
as those long lashes flutter down

Bedtime

oh the wail of the tired child
distracted all day by rain
capricious puddle jumping
early evening
examining every soaked leaf
and scattered twig

resisting pajamas
with a wriggly slither
boisterous caterwauling
about everything
lack of blanket, too much singing
milk too frothy

mother will erupt
the bronzed baby shoes
hint at the days
of newborn sleep

tomorrow will be verdant
new flowers will bloom
and hopefully a
rested little mind
will expand its branches
in the morning

Section Four

Trunk

Education

I have already consumed
so much

others' words
marched into me
boring out of pages

and what have I created?

My eyes have assimilated
their lines

I have digested
their souls

and spewed back
in analytical fervor
the meaning of their genius

Sensei! —I have cried
many times.

They left me too full
to become one of them
but now I hunger

as I chewed them
I now turn inward
a masochistic cannibal

to see what is in me
to devour

The Watcher

At the bar

Wet rag emits a moldy, bleached grime stink
from some indeterminate place behind the bar
if you're lucky enough to have a perch
on this crowded night, you have the privilege of stench
in between slugs of Boddington's and drags of Djarum
Lights

All around the patrons play the same old meat market
games:
the sidling hips, emphatic nods, sympathetic tilts
non-smokers bumming dirty little ciggies by their fifth shot
tittering too-loud laughter of fragile girls
drinking their insipid sorority shots "1—2 —3 slam-dunk"
and the men who wait to step in when their hair swings low

Bar keep, fill 'er up again, my smoke needs a companion
That rag flares out of nowhere, erasing all the evidence
spreading a new layer of putrid in the airspace
But the sex-eyed boys, the attention-starved girls are
impervious
Their senses made of steel, how can they hope to find
love?
With their mouths making noise, how can they get to
truth?

Mid-cackle some hopeful Mrs. careens backwards
manly arm juts out and closes upon manicured hand
splash of Manhattan flies towards my wrist
Barkeep, let's have that rag again
so the bar can wallow in its foul misery.

The Pleasure Seekers

All liquid was the mellow night; all night
the warmth encompassed me in aural waves;
with passionate licks of its mellifluous tongue,
the music did caress my soul and fill
me with the need to touch the souls of those
who perched around me lost in folds of sound,
and swirling clouds of thought that spun
and wove themselves into our minds as though
the tightly woven rules that run the world
unfurled, releasing us into the power
of luscious oneness with the tribal choir
as sound and touch and sight whirled into one,
so soft and free, so sensuous and pure—
so free to be the inner self, the one
that clings to childish things and random games.
Our glittering eyes, suspended living stars
requested something tangible to fill
the yearning space of our expectant vibes
which, quivering, pulsed in waves of sine sublime.
Our bodies also pulsed until we threw
ourselves into a frenzied dance that broke
the boundaries of each isolated space
and joined us, panting, laughing on the floor—
our energy expelled, we turned once more
to feel the synthesis of senses come.
The sheer desire to be consumed returned
in final sublimation by discourse.

Writing in the 21st Century
(How Penmanship Became Typing)

Roads leading upward,
Horizontally and sometimes
Downward
Lazily looping
Onwards toward peaks and valleys
The dying art
Of driving thought
With both hands at the wheel:
One to steady
And one upon the instrument of choice
This seductive dance upon paper
Made progressively archaic
By the speed of tapping
At that infinite window
A mechanical spider
Jabbing strokes in ordered lines
Crystallization beginning at fingertips
To stiffen right to the heart
Continuing on this ever desensitizing path—
Patterns of a colder nature
Transforming caresses to stabs
Feelings to emoticons
And the wild open road
To a cobweb's thread.

Oneness

Step inside the sound of the fountain
Rushhhhhhhhhhhhhhhhhhhh
Shhhhhhhhhhhhhhhhhhhhhhh
shhhhhhhhhhhhhhhhhhhhhing down
Cascading froth
                jumps
                  plops
A million white Slinkys tumble down the tiers
Leaping suicidally from last step to pool
Whitewater light
                radiates
                  exudes
Absorbs now forever
Hear no other, see no other, speak no other
But this being
Inside the light of the white
Sound

At the Entrance

At the entrance
up there with the ice cream face
slow appraisal from cultured wrinkles
weight-shifting descent
sometimes no one, just concrete
well groomed lope of vacation family
distorted little kid holds on to hand
long summer dress accompanies leashed dog
The stubby, stone wall is there
With emaciated pigeon and sharp spike

Flesh moves past this rock and metal
Flesh decays faster than stone

If time lapse sped up earthly revolution
Then we would spark and wane
Like the fragile match flame

While stone would slowly crumble
bringing both to common residue of ash.

Stop the imaginary spinning
and once again, in real time
It's only people walking in and out
through the stone entrance to a park.

Phonetic Surrender

sugar
that beautiful word
begins with a shush of reverence
for confectionary glory
then an oooh of delight
for the pleasure to come
and a gurgle in the back of the throat
confirms the craving
then a muffled ahhh
in celebration of decadence
which ends with a purr
of sweet satisfaction
shhh-uuu-ggg-ahhh-rrr

Semiprecious

Lavender Jade Buddha
Tenderly carved smooth
Milky-violet belly gleams
Enlightens my palm

Pink Quartz Rose
Innocent yet cold
Smooth pink ridges beckoning
For a warm tongue's lick

Lapis Rose
Rare dark bloom you are
No yellow rose of Texas
But midnight cowboy

Coral
Blood-red corpuscles
Ocean-moiled in reef's bosom
A heart fragmented

Fickle Inspiration

The Muse leaves me so easily—
panting after her on the shores
of the brink of my mentality,
taking with her magic words
to connect the state of the inner soul
with the outer world, leaving behind
a confused, uncaring, disconnected
creature staring into the night's gaze
in dry observation, all thoughts for now
suspended, only absorbing surroundings
almost as fuel for the Muse,
she eats my surroundings hungrily,
so that she may have strength
to pour forth the sought-after words
I need to keep me going,
yet I keep being pulled away.

The Watcher

Paris

Paris is like one long, undulating orgasm
The tremors come in images
Images with warmth and pleasure

One pulse—seductive Sacre-Coeur, mother to Montmartre
Two pulse—the banks of the Seine
long walk, river flows, cobblestones
Three pulse—mad crowd on Rue Mouffetard
choosing fruits, and vegetables, and chickens,
the narrow sloping street alive and thronging
Four pulse—on the Metro again
slithering underground in Paris
the long train thrusting through the tunnel
gliding in the warm tight enclosure

Yeah, with warmth and pleasure
receding back through the reverie of rooftops
to one cool cigarette smoked alone.

Maryjane

How often have I seen the world
through such eyes of wonder,
appreciating basic form
and rainbow color?
Come, whirlwinds of sensation
Words twist like DNA.
Running through
swift white clouds
across an azure sky
Technology looms
silver and black ahead
pathways of rings
but it smiles,
beckons, beguiles
flowing for miles and miles:
Maryjane.

Painting Sounds through Touch (My Synaesthesia)

With fingertips, dipped in colors of imagination
Conjure-woman, I trace intricate patterns on your face
Blooms spring forth in the wake of my trails
While you lay supine under my incantation

I paint what I see
Dual reciprocity:
Your smile is saturated with the pleasure of touch
And mine reflects my mind full of visions
A medium finding outlet
And a subject finding sensation

What I see is a tapestry of sound
Music fills the still space of this encounter
Each instrument my ear perceives
With a corresponding visual design
Channeled in the music's ebb and flow
Through my fingers in this massage-dance upon your
countenance
Where each touch equals vision equals sound

College Boy

Impulse impulse impulse
None left undone
Nothing left unsaid
body and mind in sync
but you get no satisfaction
your outer self
is even sated
but the inside you:
it blushes sometimes
hides often
oh you laugh
your laugh—but,
more.

Where others try to
dream away the barriers
that separate them from the world,
You
wish
for
a
little wall
You aren't unreal
just
(slightly mad?)
restless
magnet
go find a metallic mirror
and
be yourself.

Fool's Gold Love

She starts to think
With every—*plink*—that maybe it's all pointless
Charging down indifferent streets
A stream of peering faces pass
Her outlandish necklace swings
With the rhythm of each step

Its noise every sixth or seventh beat
Makes her want to hide behind buses
Retract this embarrassing statement of self
Reject him finally and all his
Sudden hits and hurtful shouts
Each step a thought to break his will
Her will—a *clink*—(a smash of glass)

Each face a stare they see right in
To her despair—*kerplunk*—she needs a drink
(He always has her share and more)
Why is her individual touch a burden now?
She loved it when she put it on this morning

But now each time the dumb thing—*clacks*—
(They burn, his slaps) she longs for his attack
To ridicule its ugliness, its invalidity
To rip it from her stupid throat
And throw it at the gutter grate
Then let her know with manly force
There's more to come than just a bruise

A worthless piece—why doesn't she just slip it off,
(Why won't he love her like her childhood dreams?)
Just let it fall there in the street

The Watcher

And never return home again?

Because she made the choice so long ago
A souvenir from that last single trip—a maiden fair
How the Mexicano laughed as she chose
The one among the colorful dangling wares
While merrily accepting Jose Cuervo shots
The one she chose was handsome, tall, and strong
How could she know that one day she'd regret

He took her love so hungrily at first
His outbursts faded into daily noise
Mere traffic in her sunny days
He doled out touch like semi precious stones
Strung carelessly and fastened with a biting clasp
(She always begged for more)

She wore her carefully chosen treasure
The night they met and made love in the last call hours
His morning coldness did nothing to deter
This play that for four years has been dragging on
And so they swing for her, the bauble and the man
From angry strain to blindfold adoration
What's garish always hovering in the wings

Street Walk Song

Headphones on your head
Replacing all the noise
With your favorite song
And all the strangers' blank stares
With a secret human kinship
Into friendly darting eyes

the sound fills up your ears and
wraps the world around you
and you're walking like a river
or the rain come down the mountain

with a perfectly cloudless heart

walking like a river
carving out the pavement
flowing through the crowds
cascading over curbs

with a perfectly cloudless heart

now the street is yellow lit and empty
cars pass slowly like endless washing machine cycles
all is calm & still except taxi drivers slash through always
my street approaches with every step I take

the sound so sweetly flowing
down the long road home.

The Watcher

Estella

Estella, bella
i miss
caressing you
making your
strings
sing
feeling
your
body
vibrate
against
my
belly
in my arms our tender love began
with my left hand i gingerly
pressed your vital points
hearing your muted stirrings
with my right, by thumb and fingertip
i walked miles of melodies
how could i have let you slip
from my inexperienced grasp?
i know i feared not ever doing you justice
i know that i've abandoned others just the same
symphonies begun yet never finished
i've left them before i ever truly got to know them
but you, my dear, are different—
fresh, you'll take me back anytime
Estella, bella
then why do you still
recline in that dusty corner,
my sweet guitar ?

Winter Woman March

she breathed the chill air on beautiful winter days
composing a path through slender trees
her thoughts sharp and clear in the sun

her breathing aligned with each footstep
inhaling for a count of two, exhaling for two
the staccato rhythm of brisk steps
moved her breath in successive bursts
in and out triumphantly

rounding out the drums of feet and winds of breath
a melody developed in her head to go along
marching down the avenue thus
she was a one-woman band
in tune with her steps, her breath, her mind
arms swaying at her sides like batons.

Section Five

Roots

Summer of '93

I.

"Confused"
She whispered
It had been her day
The tree leaves had just
said
goodbye to summer
And they browned with
golden redness.
The night girl tripped
and spilled the stars into
the sky
And so it came
But she, the other
was trapped in her
halcyon memories
Good being before
And coldness replacing
the good.
The dark
The dark
The dark
Her mumbling brain
could not grasp
She could not lift her head
to listen to hear
Life is around her
Her happiness depends
Her sexual awakening
Revel in it
She holds it precious

in her middle
Where is.......?
in my.....

II.

"Spinning O? her Treno,"
Play Dead
Let's shave our heads,
and all the rest
melt and grow
take shape all together
But the one who satisfied
her
Floats as a surreal
demigod
She wants to caress him
Visions of a flaming
sun tattoo
dance in front of her eyes
Gazes and yearns
in adoration
He stroked and caressed
Plucked gently with his thumb
The guitar was alive
She wanted to be the guitar

III.

Together
sky below them
(Is there such a
place?)
Blue light-rippling
line
Fire within
On a bus or in class

He's out there he's
right outside

IV.

"I want you,"
her mind lazily told
him.
—What?
"I said: so what are
you
listening to?"
—It's
bluesjazzsomeband
Wanna hear?
Her eyes closed
briefly,
Lips moist, lightly
parted
As he gently slipped
the device on her
A new world began.

Chimeralove

The indecisive absence
Of love was
A silent chimera
Haunting the summer

Nightmare (sonnet #1)

Could anything upset me more than that
Which doth replace the sweetness dancing in
my head at night? The horror then which sat
upon my mumbling brain and tore the thin,
the fine blue line 'twixt dark and light? I squirm.
Yet now I do perceive a certain view;
The demons which so shake my soul; the firm
and certain, real sense that got me through
the day is now a distant memory.
As Night Girl trips and spills the stars across
the sky they come and take reality
Away. A fear unknown is mental loss.
I dread the night and nothing else can soothe
But peaceful sleep these monsters to remove.

Nightmare (sonnet #2)

What anxious worm within my mind exists
which must derange the sweet stars dancing in
my head at night; this horror, then, which twists
inside my mumbling brain and tears the thin,
ethereal line 'twixt sane and mad? I squirm.
As nightfall trips and spills the stars across
the sky, delirious words explode. The firm
and certain, real sense of day is lost—
sanity is now a distant memory.
Distorted thoughts, in rapid pulsing, gibbering
spite descend and shatter the starry reverie
of night. I start to think my mind is slipping.
In coiling flesh of my malicious brain
does hope exist to see the stars again?

The Watcher

Macedonian Nocturne

A crisp black night in dark
December:
being there but not wholly
being there,
the cold cold air and black sky

> A warm soft hand, five rings
> One on each finger, silver

Concrete gray stones
rising, flat and cold.
Long walk—the bodies walk
the mouths feign talk, the
mind
remains suspended so that

> Black downy jacket, boots
> too large
> but black, A face of
> classic intensity, black hair
> flowing like some neo-
> Viking poet

the river fantasy lives on.
Dark love rushes on like the
Silent Vardar between the
cold
and concrete stones that are
its banks.

> Such curls, my length, but

The Watcher

black
Punctuation mark under red
lips
the Nosferatu prince strives
to speak my language

On its silent journey
from the crags of Sar to
Salonika
where the Aegean Sea
receives
the dark waters

the dark waters.

       my dark prince

You once stole my soul
by another river, it was black
then too, but not so desolate
and I fell under your
ancient Nosferatu spell
with one bite.

The water is foul
stories of waste and sewerage
and dirty gipsy children,
it cannot escape
from its own blackness

       cannot escape

Maybe Ohrid is a better
place
the placid lake of summer
homes

but here
it's gray, it's gray, it's gray
and black in all the times
it isn't gray.

                    You caressed my inner
                    darkness,
                    saturated my mind with all
                    its opposites, complements;
                    my light to your dark.

Nothing shines here, the stars
in the cold dark sky are
muffled—
the beauty lies only in

                    the consistency of the
                    darkness.
                    Maybe I have a better place
                    to put this kind of love.

On a cold, dead night
on the banks of the Vardar
River,

                    a cold, dead love runs its
                    course.

The Watcher

Eleven days

Eleven days of darkness
after each outburst
verbally transmitted longings
sunshine pours upon sunshine
and minutes melt into days
but there is always
the cloud of non-fulfillment
lack of instant gratification
waiting
always waiting
always wanting
raw soul
Still don't know what love is,
but emotion is.
Tender, reread over and over...
kissed and hugged
is the letter: as
person placebo
But that is not enough
ugly, black gathering ball
of darkness
sadness
desire...
Eleven days
for love
to travel
on paper

The Watcher

Photograph

The ancient pouf-and-flash
That confined their smiles in time
Faded
Yet their amusement is forever
Displayed

The Watcher

How it began

I met you
on a crystal plane.
We saw each other
as so many
fragmented pieces
The rays our hearts sent
bent
A prism of
tentative aspiration
was formed
The moon
played no role
Yet, upon a swift
boat, with
rose petals
that smelled like raspberries
and spicy cigarettes
with moist ground
we joined.
The crystal can be
taken out and
looked at
for many years.

To the Tailor

Bespectacled, your hunched form squints
at needlework in deep creased hands
pierce in, pull out, dull silver wields
a strike against decrepitude

Perhaps your finest patterns seek
the women's acquiescent gaze
your silky swatches strive to earn
their daughters' titillated praise

In ochre shades of dying light
your skill revives an antique gown
a bride will dance her wedding night
while you work on it solitude.

Porch Summers

When we were children,
Grandpa sat, looking tough
Each stifling summer
While we toasted to his years
With Cokes.

When we dated,
The porch swing swung awkwardly
With our first kisses
The songs of crickets competing
With cicadas.

Sheltered from amber-glowing stars
We watched on still, hot nights
Tree branches frozen
Against the sky like lighting
Praying for the rain.

When we left,
Grandpa's spirit nodded from the swing
Well-worn were the steps
That guided us into the world
With fond memories.

The Death of the Captive Bear

the death of the captive bear
Alone
found ruined yet like sleeping
desiring winter to end

for days he wandered in vain
Alone
between the preservation's boundaries
foraging for food

the berries were trampled by tourists
Alone
and in groups allowed to hunt
desiring trophies for their walls

for control had lapsed in the region
Alone
the bear found himself
desiring a partner

the death of the captive bear
Alone
found ruined yet like sleeping
desiring winter to end.

Tragedy in the Snow

snow was falling
when the goose
found his mate
just after the gunshot
resounded in the ice-colored sky
he stood beside her frozen wings

with wrath he quacked
spittle flying from his beak
but all around him
the unkind snowflakes fell
each unique as each blood droplet
blasted from his lover's down

panting and footfalls
soon heralded
the hunter-murderers' approach
with one last glossy glance
of rueful beady eye
the survivor trudged away

Note to Self

She's a little girl
in a big girl shell
the thoughts she has
would make anyone else go mad
she dwells and dwells
and thinks once more
never happy
with her conclusions
is it this self speaking?
or is it that one?

Poor little girl
I look down from
above
and hope for the best
but only in retrospect
does the truth
become apparent
I feel sorry for her
if only she could
see the present
with the benefit of hindsight

She rides life high
and suddenly
she gets confused,
gets off a little dizzy
and realizes she was
on the wrong ride
and doesn't know where
she is;
wrong highway exit

The Watcher

why the confusion?

Little girl, little girl
go to college
don't over-think
she's going to make all the wrong choices
I can feel it
I wish I could help her
I don't know what to do
maybe she needs time to herself
but isolation breeds subjectivity
Why must there be so
many levels of thinking?
why can't she have one
rational plateau of thought
from where all of her
decisions come?

My sweet little girl;
open your eyes
realize it's your life
no one can make you do
anything you don't want to
resignation is not the easy decision
maybe the way to go
is the exciting defiant way of life
I bet she wishes
she had a muse
but I know she needs
to see for herself

Little, little, young girl
can't separate
the parental her from
the impulse her
will she thank them later?

The Watcher

Such a thin line she walks
maybe she longs for safety
all this recklessness is
making her nervous
and crazy and weird
and scared

She finds relief in simplicity
yet thrives on excitement
she'd better get a little of both
when she's older
how grown up is she really?
how can it be measured?
She's so lost.
I think what she
really wants
is ....

THE PRAIRIE

Three children, laying in the carpet of—
THE PRAIRIE
The one, tall and fair, with soul
as pure as the flowers wound in his hair
by the other two.
Was it love that drove them here?
Suppression at home.
"I'm... so happy, " she said
And gave them each a kiss.
She kissed the ground, wished for a bunny rabbit
and did a little dance.
Her highness sat up—
"In my forest, birds sing freely."
"Find me in me, I am not them!"
But the girls, locked in a mind game, did not hear.
As they pondered the bladeness of the grass
It came sniffing towards them.
"Oh, hello, elf."
He was enchanted, "Can I touch you?"
That is how it all began.
Unfettered now, I think he escaped.
It's his forest now.

Tribute to a Best Friend

I don't want to think of you
In terms of board games:
You have power over me.
I don't want to evaluate you
based on your questions:
You make me feel guilty.
All I want to do is love you
In a way a best friend could
And despite all the doubts and fears
take you for who you are.
Your existence has a simple meaning
It's not what you do
that makes you special
you have a deeper shade of understanding
of me and of the world.
You use your knowledge.
You amaze me with your mind.
It has such a capacity...
For love? For variety?
For things that are constantly
beyond your reach?
You suffer
Yet you live on a different plane
You can SO rise above the rest,
Overcome your limits
and your limitations
I don't know whether you
are better off than me;
I probably never will
such is the way you present things.
but remember this, dear one:
You are always my most basic necessity.

Thanks, Jim

Words,
the ancient lizard sings
Dakota Badlands echo
Golden glittering road listens
Words,
poet struggles
to find
just the right spoken chord
The lizard speaks
in minor sixths
Calling upon strains of lost love
But struggling to find
his own voice
among the inspirations
Vast nature echoes his cry
in a crescendo
the poet always
tries to reach
Words,
seem inadequate.